Gallery Books
Editor: Peter Fallon
LAKE GENEVA

Gerald Dawe

LAKE GENEVA

Gallery Books

Lake Geneva
is first published
simultaneously in paperback
and in a clothbound edition
on 24 April 2003.

The Gallery Press
Loughcrew
Oldcastle
County Meath
Ireland

*All rights reserved. For permission
to reprint or broadcast these poems,
write to The Gallery Press.*

© Gerald Dawe 2003

ISBN 1 85235 341 4 (*paperback*)
      1 85235 342 2 (*clothbound*)

A CIP catalogue record for this book
is available from the British Library.

The Gallery Press acknowledges the financial assistance
of An Chomhairle Ealaíon / The Arts Council, Ireland.

Contents

Stormy Weather *page* 11
Midsummer Report 12
The Interface 13
Laughter and Forgetting 14
1922 16
Perspective at Slieve Donard 17
Two Portraits
   IAIN CRICHTON SMITH 18
   ELEANOR DUNCAN 19
Snap 20
The Buzz 21
The Dead Zone 22
Silent Partners 23
Siesta 24
Delta 25
Raccoons 26
Text Messages 27
A Moving World
  AT HOME 28
  THE JAZZ CLUB 29
  STRANGE MEETING 30
  THE MIDDLE OF ENGLAND 31
  ROOM WITH A VIEW 32
  FIFTY/FIFTY 33
Distraction 34
The Fox 36
Homecoming 37
Pet Days 38
The Transparent Man 40
Night and Morning 41
An Evening in the Country 42
Dolphins 43
Lake Geneva 44

Acknowledgements 51

for Dorothea

'Moonshine and Lion are left to bury the dead.'
— A Midsummer Night's Dream

Stormy Weather

How come you hear the foghorn of a ship
when there isn't any?
You should be above in the attic
within sight of the bay.

The trees roll into themselves.
Early today, with a mist rising off
the lake, deer emerged,
like shadows, into the sunlight.

Unquestionable, momentary,
three or four of them stood,
and for once in a long while
you were no longer in thrall.

The clouds alter course
and from one minute to another
it's hard to tell what the day will bring.
I sit in the bay window,

butterflies trip and trace
amidst bushes of red berry and acacia.
One will cross the newly mown lawn,
taking up the full picture,

bare as a leaf blown crossways.
The trees are my horizon
and behind them more clouds
altering course.

Midsummer Report

The smokeless chimney sprouts scutch grass
and the entry has bits and pieces of furniture
at one end or the other — the inside of a fridge,
a couch on its side, hedge clippings.

Here and there a light goes on or off
in a landing, a hallway. The back room's
the same unchanging view of cars
parked higgledy-piggledy on the footpath.

Between the trees, the houses
become dusky outlines —
the bricked-up fireplace, the bedside locker,
the converted attic, the rooms for let.

Walking after midnight, watch your step.
Things have changed around here, no mistake.

The Interface

'The lights are going on in towns that no longer exist'
and in the districts we never knew we lived in
between the cemetery where turncoat rebels
are said to be buried and the narrow road north.

In the parlours of the very few who stayed put
the *Telegraph*'s folded, the curtains in perfect order
and the radio putters in the background.
Good news is rarely expected.

The kids are well grown and gone
to Scotland, Canada, the West Country,
and for all the time they spent together
little remains the same:

pound shops and discount bars and fast food joints,
and even the church is up for sale.
See. What did I tell you? It is the case
that the biggest fall is the fall from grace.

Laughter and Forgetting

The wine store has gone lilac
   and where the Jaffé Memorial
stands in a forlorn green
   the Lagan glides by.
Girl rowers scull in
   and out of the winter sun.
It's cold enough, making your way
   up Ridgeway Street.
The houses on both sides
   change hands each year —
broken banisters, the ancient
   skylight, *Ireland Saturday Night*s
at the back of the water tank.
   Newspaper shops, home bakeries,
a restaurant in what
   was somebody's front room,
and the attic that's a store
   has initials carved on
the window's leaded flashing
   that no one knows anything about —
except maybe you walking down
   town as the school kids
head out to the traffic lights.
   Old folk sit in the Gardens
among the deepening shades
   and over at the Bookshop
set texts for the first years
   are piled high. *Indie* music
blasts out from the Students' Union
   while those unwelcome stand
at the low wall waiting admission.
   There's Riesling bottles down
the back of the Lombard Café
   and there's empty cans of Harp

and flagons of scrumpy
   dumped in King William's Park.
Do you remember? Do you remember?
   Do you remember, what?
The hillsides are glorious
   and that's as good as it gets.

1922

Above the Shalimar Takeaway
in the border country a young boy
peers out through the curtains.
He must do this every Sunday

when the Expressway stops
for only a minute
to take the regulars on board
and then we're off again.

The builder's date gives *1922*
but window by bricked-up window
the ragged flags flutter about his head;
the long awaited return to better days.

Perspective at Slieve Donard

In the hotel room at five in the morning
there wasn't a sound and it was so dark
I thought this is what it'll be like
when the heart races cease and the blink
of an eye freezes over and then doesn't exist.
By six, sure enough, light filters in.

∽

Breaks in the sky give more light
that picks out a man and his dog
as they cover the strand, white horses
and the mountains behind all profile.
Cars flash by on the headland,
houses fallen in are knocked.

∽

From this height, close up,
a spider's web is like the rigging of a ship.

Two Portraits

IAIN CRICHTON SMITH

To think that this could be you
making faces outside the wackiest shop in town,
to think that this was you and not the ubiquitous Murdo;
to think that this was you in the schoolmaster's suit

ambling onto stage at an awkward age;
to think that this was you paying particular attention
to the exact moment — whatever it was —
in the fearful station,

in the deserted village and the council estate,
in the unforgiving city and the shopping mall,
in the secluded bungalow and the brooding church
you knew like the back of your hand.

I think of you now in the clearing,
the light has reached a pack of *Gold Bond*,
a small whisky and a glass of water
the likes of which you haven't seen before.

ELEANOR DUNCAN

Out of nowhere they appear —
these tall women in fox fur, luminous faces.
What they had been through I never found out.
Childless, in the main, spinsters, widows,
they were unimpressed by grief,
the body's decline, the loquacious man friend.

I heard in wonderment their voices
downstairs, except, that is, for Eleanor,
alone in her father's house — the door
closed on the good front room, the pantry
sparse and the garden in tiptop condition.

With hymnal and church service
she managed until the end
and took with her the silence of a Sunday,
the distant shout as late evening light
played on the isolated cul-de-sac and the belief
that this was all there was ever meant to be.

Snap

Emigrant family leaving Derry, 1930s

If I had known I would have kept this picture
on the mantelpiece of each home we had.
The two of them could hardly stand still, her shy
as anything and the young lad held fast
to his daddy's hand. Our tickets were in the other.

The day was cool enough, a mist settled
and the engines churned and churned. It felt
as if we were on land and the land on either side
was distant, foreign. I couldn't believe we were going.
The kids looked this way and that until the open sea,
nothing but the sea, and I thought my heart would break.

The Buzz

I was in my cabin
by the shore
wondering about a coffee
when on comes CNN
and this time
the footage takes us
to the side of a hill,
two-storied red tile
houses, with chicken coops.
And, from the '50s,
pick-up trucks
and it's all in flames —

but there's no one there
except the camera man
and before you know it
we're switched to
a 'Glam' band on *The Beat*
and the girl's beautiful
smiling face is soundless,
but what does it matter,
she's in New York, Berlin,
or somewhere and then
that shot's done
and we're off again —

smoking away like mad.

The Dead Zone

Yainnis shows us around the dead zone
   at the dead of night.
Boy soldiers peer out of alleyways
   and fortifications
which zig this way and that
   along the border.
A statue to the great and mighty
   dominates an ancient square.
'This is Greek; that is Turk.'

∽

Only in the nether world
   of water and crap is the island
at peace. Gays hang out
   on Hermes Street where the killings
started decades ago
   and in the derelict rooming houses
by an empty mosque
   whoever lives there now keeps it secret.
'This is Greek; that is Turk.'

∽

A cloudy sky —
   sun burns the backs
of the season's first arrivals
   who have weathered the night flight
from Bradford or Essex.
   Undeterred, a couple
anoint each other
   at the swimming pool.
'This is Greek; that is Turk.'

Silent Partners

for the Costigans

A little lizard comes to visit us
   in our temporary house.
It sits in the harsh sunlight,
   the pulse of life beats in its neck
as it shimmers like sand on the beach.
   The cocky head tweaks
one way and another before
   it scoots into the cave of a wall,
the jasmine-flowering universe.

෴

Bizarrely 'Lara's Theme'
   from an ice-cream float
on its regular route to the village . . .
   Distant eerie sounds enchant
from a childhood away of Sundays
   when the signature tunes for
Z Cars or *Maigret* filter through
   the shadowy avenues of Seaview
and we too taste the exotic.

෴

The bells of Victoria clang loudest
   and even the kids'
constant play can't drown them out:
   'Mama,' the French boy calls, 'Mama',
while the rest of us smile.
   The late afternoon sexual heat
glows off our older bodies.
   Fathers, mothers, husbands, wives,
silent partners in each other's lives.

Siesta

They are moving the furniture about
in hell. Around this time each day
the scraping and shifting begins.

Or else, in the ever-so-bright afternoon,
the idiot kid makes sure we all hear
the western or soap opera that blares
out over the de Chirico street.

Even as I speak the dark rooms
are filled with the dubbed action films
we may as well all be watching.

Leave it to me, he seems to be saying,
when you awaken from your slumbers,
I will recall the human world
you thought you had escaped.

Delta

Walking the dog one afternoon
Ron spots at the lakeshore
an old Vietnamese woman fishing,
her bicycle left by a tree.

This, however, is Switzerland.

She is at the delta of a river
that goes on forever where her
village sits at the back of her mind,
and the silence she hears

is of a completely different kind
from the hushed busyness of this
place which she's made her own
in the time it takes to catch a fish.

Raccoons

Behind the lids of my eyes
the sun turns blood red.
Islands sit blankly
in a moleskin sea.
'The sun puts the fire out.'

In Vancouver the fiery
eyes of raccoons
came out of the darkness
like little devils
to hiss and mock
and jeer. No matter,
rest easy. Enjoy
the heat of the day.

Text Messages

Sloe gin. Single malt. The occasional grappa.
Wine from Lorenzo, wine from the valley. Marsala.

Open all the doors. Open all the windows, the sun's caught
up with us in our mountainy retreat.

The arrow garden defies the landslides, the wind
and the rain. Your home is built on solid ground.

The poignancy of driftwood, the cloud formation.
Snow on the mountaintops and, on the lake, drifting swans.

And then, before you know it, the windows shuttered,
the rain spills down through brilliant sunshine.

All the shadows are angles you half imagine
in the actual rise and fall of this home from home.

Amidst the farmhouses and vine groves,
the dark valley, you knock the light off.

At the airport you go your separate ways.
Who will turn back a second time to wave?

A Moving World

'Here, now, oh, Wellingborough, thought I, learn a lesson, and never forget it. The world, my boy, is a moving world; it never stands still; and its sands are forever shifting.'
— Herman Melville, *Redburn*

AT HOME

When I was young I'd wake sometimes
to a hot pillow and bedraggled clothes,
draining the night for air.
And at first light I'd hear
the men start to move around the street,
senior clerk, City and Guild apprentice.

I'd stay off from school imagining the hubbub
but by mid-morning the quiet had settled
as women took to the shops
and old men walked about,
callers at empty houses, waiting for lunch.
I'd drift off and let the world pass by.

THE JAZZ CLUB

It's 1960 or thereabouts in the terrace
of seven houses, upper northside,
the blackout blinds still up,
but things are steadily improving.
Shops stay open late, the light
falls in rectangles from the windows.

Trolley buses clang and clank,
the mill of people going to movies,
meetings, dances, to the boat,
to the club, to church, and to Ella.
The only thing my mother says
when she comes back home
is 'I'm sent'.

STRANGE MEETING

I was reading Barzini's *The Italians*,
the chapter on cracked Mussolini,
and started to think of Rome, women
looking down from their roof gardens and balconies,
little windows where they'd been
redding up, when the noise of scooters
and horns and cars racing about
eased, and the next thing, for a split second,
you appeared, white shirt and dark pants,
the bulky head and wavy hair of my father.

'Stranger, your likeness is other than what I saw before',
though not a word was said.

THE MIDDLE OF ENGLAND

for Iarla

I don't know what possessed me
sitting in the kitchen one overcast
August day, listening to cricket
on the radio. It's overcast there
in the middle of England,
and a car alarm beeps away.

But the commentary is hypnotic
though I haven't a clue
what it all means —
'through the covers', 'deep square',
'on the boundary', before we're told
they anticipate rain.

ROOM WITH A VIEW

Up the side of the mountain,
like a trail for mountain climbers,
the winding elevated cable takes hold.
Occasionally, too, out of the blue,

voices in conversation —
a mother and child, neighbours,
the endless chattering of birds,
then the mighty generator kicks in.

Lights pop on in the helter-skelter village;
sound system, satellite dish and American freezer.
Of all places I will remember this place
when they take me out, feet first.

FIFTY/FIFTY

In the 'hours of obscurity' before sunlight
I sit down to breakfast —
all 'jumble and confusion' is right.

The first to make a move are wired for sound,
shoulder power-books. They must get
the same train Monday to Friday.

Not so you or I approaching fifty!
The odd trip here and there — Paris, Italy —
and, when the mood takes, an afternoon movie.

For you, working for the government;
for me, college kids on the move.
Such times ahead.

Distraction

I wander around the last place I had —
the private gardens I could look out on,

awaiting proofs or a letter.
My poor mother who misunderstood it all.

Paris was fun. I knocked about a bit
but deep in my heart of hearts

I knew all along that I had to get back
to the valleys of an imagined people:

the twists and turns of their language,
the girl whose shoulder brushed mine

and whose undisclosed body drove me
to distraction when I sat on the rocks,

the black edge of the north island
in front, the bay almost too blue.

In the early hours I walk by the quays
and yards of the Steamship Company.

A dog ferrets through the hotel's rubbish
the local lad, pale as a ghost, dumped

last night out of sight, betwixt and between
my leaving and my return

to the south county districts
where it's neither night and not quite day.

Kids talk to themselves
in doorways full of cartons and cans.

Pages of newspapers wrap about their feet
but they don't notice. A fawn-like girl,

hunched and jiggy, empties a white vial
and tosses it aside.

∽

The shopping centre is floodlit like a stadium
and the chimneys of the generating station flash red.

The streetlights are bright tonight
as night falls on the piers, on the coal harbour,

on the urban villas and on the dimmed descent
of the last flight home

to the terraces, parks and avenues
in the shadows of all these years.

Listen hard enough and you will just about
make out in the gathering breeze

a wrought-iron gate clunk by the stone steps
which lead up towards my old flat

where a black cat halts and stares
at whatever it imagines is there.

The Fox

after a painting by John Luke

I am stepping out to meet you
from the crazy world he has made.

Just think for a minute
that when I hit the floor before you

the hair will stand at the back of your neck —
the attendant who knows me

only too well or the lady who allowed
all this to take place

will turn, shocked, when I shake
myself, and the voluptuous scene

with those birds, whatever they are,
and burst through the clouds of your living room

or the abstract museum,
and make everything happen for real this time.

Homecoming

'Two doves,' she said on the phone,
'have just landed in the garden.

When I went out they rose
in such a flurry it was as if

I hadn't really seen them.'
'Doves, not pigeons?'

'Doves, I tell you, they were
doves. Two of them.'

Pet Days

in memory of Tom Long

The bay tree glimmers in the bright moonlight.
The shed, an outpost left far behind, sags,
and the silver birches, three of them,
are ungainly without a leaf.

The trellises rattle: old pots, a park bench,
the garden seat; and our clothes flap upside down
where Misha sleeps in the shadow
of her high stone wall. Houses, offices now,

are all the more silent. Nothing stirs
by the flip charts, the Year Round Planner,
except for computer graphics that twirl
in semi-darkness. The spring water dispenser

is a goldfish bowl.
The security systems are quiet tonight,
quiet as the grave in the moonlight
which superintends everything:

the ugly gash of the half-filled skip,
the arum lilies, his pride and joy,
the exciting new development, final phase,
the yachts tied up on the foreshore, their masts

clacking like castanets, the 4WDs
and the run-arounds sitting pretty —
so by mid-morning in the windy station,
ear-pierced, nose-pierced, head-shaven

detox kids in their thin sports gear
stare down the tracks at twenty years,
and the eyes dart, not seeing you or me
in the eggshell light that's everywhere.

The Transparent Man

He lives in a house of shoes, women's shoes,
strapless, backless shoes, high-heeled, flat
for walking. Chunky, slender, petite,
they lie about the place in dark corners,
under the tables, up narrow flights of stairs,
abandoned but not forlorn, sleeping it off.

In the bath tub, discarded tights,
a blouse, slacks, underclothes from last night's
undressing. The hair conditioners in a row
with little brushes, eyeliners, combs,
and, caught within the mirror's garden,
a man appears, or thinks he does,
re-arranges things as best he can,
and mindful of his trespass quickly goes.

Night and Morning

I hear her shower, the water spills.
She moves, draws the curtain rail, towels,
her feet pad about in the smallest room,
life and soul, all of her, overhead; unseen.

Haunch, thigh, hip, jaw line —
like a Buddha before me.
Breast plate, shoulder blade,
your lips in flight confirm.

The amber streetlight's still ablaze
but you are miles away —
only cliff face and the empty beach
as far as the eye can see.

An Evening in the Country

for Olwen

Their children run free in the adjoining field
where an abandoned car sits in a heap.
I am cutting back dead branches from a tree.

A tractor edges along our common boundary.
That would be Tuam over there, but I still can't tell
for certain the direction I am facing.

A Child of Prague floats in its red
alabaster cloak; creamery lorries arrive at dawn,
and there is a man who sits by the grave

of his young wife beseeching her to come home.
The hedges bristle with cobwebs and dew,
bramble swings out from a collapsed wall.

I hack my way through, clearing the garden.
The children's voices rise and fall;
we lift up our heads for a second and listen.

A magpie cackles, its dusty tail up in arms
with this rook circling overhead. Does one know
the other by wingspan, the gimp of its beak?

Beneath me, lost for words, you play.
It's coming on evening in the country,
swallows showing off in the lucid light.

Dolphins

'For the people of antiquity the dolphins were symbols of the soul's liberation from its earthly body.' — H G Wunderlich

The blood surges like an ocean swell.
The skull, the inner ear, the cavern's echo
an ultrasound.

I am disappearing into a wall.
Forgive me, I want to say.
It'll be over in a trice.

My life is there before me —
its bits and pieces fit
like a jigsaw puzzle.

Look. This is how it all begins,
and ends, of course,
a map of real places:

kidney, liver, spleen,
the tried and tested joints,
the scars that shine,

the transparent flesh,
the pumps, the unwinding clock,
the damage limitation,

the unsubstantiated marrow,
the rough bone, the soul stuff.
Dolphins have visited the bay,

the closest they've been sighted
in ages. Ghosts returning.
Hey, over here. Over here.
What about me? I want to say.

Lake Geneva

'Have we vanquished an enemy? None but ourselves. Have we gained success? That word means nothing here.'
— George Mallory, *Alpine Journal* (1918)

1

It's near midnight,
about me the mountains
remain intact,
rain sweeps across

the manicured lawns
of formidable *chateaux*
down to Lake Geneva
where the good people

walk their dogs.
The weather's inclement.
In *pension* and apartment
the very old refuse

to give in — hardy souls
who ended up here
like the white-haired girl
behind half curtains

feeding her Siamese cat
in a balancing act
between high window
and the long drop below.

2

Everything's in its place —
a tin can or bottle
would spell trouble
here on the lakeshore.

In the downpour,
I can hardly see before me
the excellent inn of the *Trois Couronnes*
where Daisy Miller in muslin

draws near, or imagine
the dark old city
at the other end
of this most silent lake.

3

From the night sky
planes prepare for landing.
The lake is luminous now
but not a word is heard

from the immaculate
living- and bedroom, the hallway,
the underground car park,
the narrow balcony with its

potted unspilling flowers
closed up for the night.
Is there anyone there?
What's going on? I want to know.

4

The dog on its leash
moves out of the sun.
Without a by-your-leave
two horses *clip-clop, clip-clop*

beneath my window;
a car heads into town.
Business is business
after all.

The man opposite,
whom I haven't met,
speaks into a mobile phone.
Is he Romanian, a Serbo-Croat?

The light behind him
is a flickering screen.
The kids blast out MTV:
the same the whole world over.

5

And for some reason I think
of the fluorescent evening
at Shaftesbury Square,
1974 or thereabouts.

A body's slumped
down a back lane.
The police van
turns in, slits for windows,

past unnoticed slogans
to the long war
at the Cobbles Bar.
'And where are you for?'

'Home, sir.' 'Hurry on then.'
(It's as if you're not there.)
The gutted off-licence,
the boarded-up bookshop,

the cavernous hotel
of Silver City.
The river sweats
and the embankments

are blind to our footsteps.
On Sunnyside Street
moonlight, and the darky
darky night that follows.

6

But not here,
not here. The steamer
stops on its way
around the lakeshore

at Vevey, Montreux,
Chateau de Chillon.
Byron and Shelley
are warbling still

to one another until
the storm that nearly
drowns them abates,
and the History man,

Edward Gibbon,
after laying down his pen
is taking a stroll
in the garden at Lausanne.

The Alps at my fingertips,
the lake a dream,
and the terraces trim
as they've always been.

Acknowledgements

Versions of some of these poems have appeared in *Attic, Birdsuit, College Green, Honest Ulsterman, Icarus, The Irish Times, Irish University Review, Journal of Irish Studies, Metre, Oxford Magazine, Poetry Ireland Review, ROPES, The Shop, Translation Ireland, The Backyards of Heaven* (eds. Stephanie McKenzie and John Ennis) *Interpreting Synge* (ed. Nicholas Grene), *The Living Stream: A Festschrift for Theo Dorgan* (ed. Niamh Morris), *A Conversation Piece,* (eds. Adrian Rice and Angela Reid), *Company* (with Noel Connor) and in the exhibition *Images and Reflections* (The Linen Hall Library, Belfast) to whom kind acknowledgement is made. The author also acknowledges the financial support of An Chomhairle Ealaíon/ The Arts Council, the Department of Foreign Affairs and The British Council. Special thanks for all their help to Ron Ewart and Toni O'Brien Johnson.

Murdo is a manic figure invented by Iain Crichton Smith, the Scottish poet.